Conrad K. Butler

THE WORLD OF FIRE TRUCKS

Conrad K.
PUBLISHING WAW

Argentinian fire truck

THE DAILY WORK OF THE NEW FIRE BRIGADE SHIFT STARTS WITH MANDATORY PROCEDURES: CARRYING OUT CHECKS OF RESPIRATORY PROTECTIVE EQUIPMENT, PROTECTIVE CLOTHING AND PERSONAL DOCUMENTS THAT ARE NEEDED TO IDENTIFY A PERSON IF HE OR SHE DIES.

Australian fire truck

DID YOU KNOW?

IN MOST CASES, FIREFIGHTERS WORK ON A "DAY ON DUTY, TWO DAYS OFF" PATTERN, BUT SOME BRIGADES WORK 3–4 DAYS IN A ROW FOR 10–12 HOURS. IF THERE IS AN EXCEPTIONAL SITUATION, FIREFIGHTERS CAN WORK CONTINUOUSLY FOR MORE THAN ONE DAY.

Austrian fire truck

IT IS BELIEVED THAT FOR THE FIRST TIME PEOPLE STARTED TO FORM BRIGADES TO FIGHT FIRES IN ENGLAND, AND IT WAS AN INITIATIVE OF INSURANCE COMPANIES WHO WANTED TO LIMIT LOSSES IN DISASTERS. IT IS NOT KNOWN EXACTLY, BUT PROBABLY THE FIRST FIREMEN APPEARED IN 1722.

Brazilian fire truck

DID YOU
KNOW?

THERE IS A STEREOTYPE THAT DANGEROUS WORK CAN ONLY BE DONE BY MEN, BUT IN FACT THE FIRST FEMALE FIREFIGHTER WAS MOLLY WILLIAMS, WHO ENTERED THE SERVICE IN THE EARLY 19TH CENTURY. AFTER SOME TIME, SEPARATE BRIGADES WERE CREATED, IN WHICH ONLY WOMEN WORKED.

NATIONAL GUARD
FIRE

Canadian fire truck

DID YOU KNOW?

THE FIRE BRIGADE UNIFORMS ARE MADE OF A SPECIAL MATERIAL THAT CAN WITHSTAND TEMPERATURES UP TO 1,200°C (2,192°F). IN ADDITION, IT PROTECTS AGAINST THE EFFECTS OF CONCENTRATED ACIDS AND BASES. THANKS TO THESE PROPERTIES OF THE UNIFORM, FIREFIGHTERS CAN SAVE PEOPLE FROM BURNING HOUSES.

Chinese fire truck

DID YOU KNOW?

IN THE FIRE STATION, THE SLIDE POLE IS NOT FOR BEAUTY. IN FACT, IT IS NEEDED TO LEAVE THE FLOOR AS QUICKLY AS POSSIBLE, BECAUSE CARS AND EQUIPMENT ARE USUALLY LOCATED ON THE GROUND FLOOR OF THE BUILDING, AND PEOPLE STAY ON THE UPPER FLOOR. THE POLES HAVE BEEN USED FOR ABOUT 140 YEARS.

French fire truck

DID YOU KNOW?

THE WORK OF FIREFIGHTERS IS NOT ONLY DANGEROUS, BUT ALSO HARD IN THE LITERAL SENSE OF THE WORD, BECAUSE RESCUERS HAVE TO CARRY FROM 5 TO 30 KG. IT ALL DEPENDS ON WHAT THE UNIFORM IS MADE OF AND WHAT EQUIPMENT THEY USE. CONSIDERING THESE FACTORS, WE UNDERSTAND THAT ONLY PHYSICALLY PREPARED PEOPLE ARE SUITABLE FOR WORK IN THE FIRE DEPARTMENT.

German fire truck

AFTER RECEIVING THE FIRE SIGNAL, THE BRIGADE HAS ONLY A FEW MINUTES TO PUT ON THE UNIFORM, TAKE THE EQUIPMENT AND BE IN THE CAR. TO DO THIS, THEY KEEP THEIR THINGS IN A SPECIAL WAY, FOR EXAMPLE, THEY PRE-ROLL THEIR PANTS AND TUCK THEM INTO THEIR SHOES.

Greek fire truck

A STANDARD FIRE TRUCK HAS A TANK THAT HOLDS APPROXIMATELY 2,350 LITERS (620 GALLONS) OF WATER. IF ONLY ONE HOSE IS CONNECTED, THIS AMOUNT OF WATER IS USED IN 7.5 MINUTES. EACH CAR HAS SPECIAL PUMPS DESIGNED FOR QUICK REPLENISHMENT OF WATER SUPPLIES. IT CAN BE CONNECTED TO A HYDRANT OR TO PUMP WATER FROM AN OPEN TANK.

Indian fire truck

IN MOST COUNTRIES, IF A HUMAN STARTED A FIRE, THEY MAY NOT FACE CHARGES, AND THE FIREFIGHTERS THEMSELVES MAY BE UNDER INVESTIGATION. AFTER THE FIRE IS EXTINGUISHED, A TEAM OF EXPERTS ARRIVES AT THE SCENE TO DETERMINE THE SOURCE OF THE FIRE AND DRAW UP AN ACT OF LEGALITY OF EXTINGUISHING THE FIRE. THEY ASSESS WHETHER THE TEAM WORKED PROPERLY AND DID NOT CAUSE AVOIDABLE DAMAGE.

Japanese fire truck

AN INTERESTING FACT FOR SOME PEOPLE MAY BE THE FACT THAT FIREFIGHTERS ARE RESPONSIBLE NOT ONLY FOR EXTINGUISHING FIRES, BUT ALSO FOR A NUMBER OF OTHER TASKS. WHAT? THEY HELP IN EXTRICATING INJURED PEOPLE FROM VEHICLES AND REMOVING HAZARDOUS SUBSTANCES FROM THE ROAD. THEY TAKE ACTIONS TO PROTECT RESIDENTS, PROPERTY AND INFRASTRUCTURE DURING NATURAL DISASTERS SUCH AS FLOODS, STORMS OR STRONG WINDS.

Mexican fire truck

DID YOU KNOW?

IN THE FIRST YEARS OF OPERATION OF THE FIRE BRIGADE, ITS UNITS DID NOT HAVE MUCH FUNDING, AND FIREFIGHTERS CONSISTED MAINLY OF VOLUNTEERS. INTERESTINGLY, THEY SAVED MONEY ON EVERYTHING, INCLUDING THE PAINT FOR FIRE TRUCKS. AND SINCE THE RED ONE WAS THE CHEAPEST, CARS WERE DECORATED WITH IT. SUCH A BRIGHT COLOR ALSO HELPED FIRE TRUCKS STAND OUT FROM OTHER, MAINLY BLACK, VEHICLES.

Spanish fire truck

DID YOU KNOW?

IN MANY COUNTRIES, PEOPLE VOLUNTARILY JOIN FIRE BRIGADES. IN MOST CASES, THEY ARE ORGANIZED WHERE THE GOVERNMENT CANNOT FINANCE THE WORK OF THE RESCUE BRIGADE. FOR EXAMPLE, IN CHILE THERE ARE SEVERAL THOUSAND VOLUNTEER FIREFIGHTERS WHO PAY MONTHLY CONTRIBUTIONS AND UNDERGO SPECIAL TRAINING. IN SOME COUNTRIES, ONLY PEOPLE WITH HIGHER EDUCATION CAN BE FIREFIGHTERS.

British fire truck

DID YOU KNOW?

MOVIES ABOUT FIREFIGHTERS SHOW FIREFIGHTERS SKILLFULLY MOVING AROUND A BURNING BUILDING AND FINDING VICTIMS OR A WAY OUT, BUT IN REALITY IT'S THE OTHER WAY AROUND. IN A BURNING HOUSE FILLED WITH SMOKE, NOTHING CAN BE SEEN, AND AMIDST THE ROARING AND CRACKLING FIRE, NOTHING CAN BE HEARD, NOT EVEN PEOPLE SCREAMING. THAT'S WHY RESCUERS MOVE CAREFULLY IN BURNING ROOMS, PRACTICALLY "BY TOUCH".

American fire truck

FINALLY, NOT ONLY AN INTERESTING FACT ABOUT THE FIRE BRIGADE, BUT ALSO A WARNING. UNJUSTIFIED USE OF EMERGENCY NUMBERS IS INADVISABLE AND MAY RESULT IN SERIOUS LEGAL CONSEQUENCES. IN MOST COUNTRIES, THIS CAN RESULT IN A FINE OR EVEN IMPRISONMENT. IN ADDITION, THE PERSON RESPONSIBLE FOR SUCH AN OFFENSE MAY BE CHARGED WITH THE COSTS ASSOCIATED WITH ORGANIZING THE RESCUE OPERATION.

Check also:

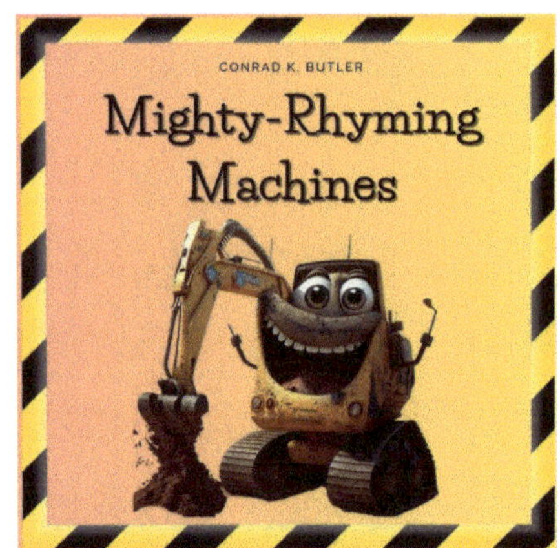

and much more!

f /conradpublishing